A Childs Book of Trees Through Po

To Evia

♡ M. Power.

A Childs Book Of Trees Through Poetry

By Margaret Power

A Childs Book of Trees Through Poetry

A Childs Book of Trees Through Poetry

A Childs Book of Trees Through Poetry

A Childs Book of Trees Through Poetry

Ogham Alphabet

Have you heard of Ogham?

It is an ancient alphabet,

Ireland is its home,

Your attention it will get,

Each letter in it,

Represents a different tree,

Many trees do fit,

Oak is Dair so it holds the letter D,

B is for Birch, but its called Beith,

Hazel is called Coll and so it gets the C.

If you search on google then i'm sure you will see.

Maple

In Canada they tap the Maple,

Well before its April,

They take its yummy syrup,

For all the world to cheer up,

Covering our pancakes,

And adding into bakes,

Sweet sticky honey,

From the maple tree.

RED MAPLE (Acer rubrum.)

Hazel

My Hazel tree,

Provides a lot of greenery,

I collected lots of nuts,

Aaand there are some buts.

Each time I did crack,

There was nothing to unpack!

No little nutty treat,

In there for me to eat!

So I have considered,

Perhaps there is a wizard,

Maybe the squirrel chief,

Is the magic thief?!

Ash

Who knew how many,

Health benefits there'd be,

From just one tree,

Its seed is called a key,

Twin branches grow oppositely,

Leaves grow in pairs to form a canopy,

Jet black buds mark it easily,

So anyone can see,

When they have an Ash tree.

(In Norse mythology, It's also the world tree)

Horse Chesnut

In the yard to conquer,

I collected the conker,

The best I chose to play,

The rest left for another day,

Tied in a bag,

Hooked on a snag,

All through the winter I'd forgotten,

The bag I'd thought was rotten,

But I opened it to see,

A surprise for me!

They'd begun to sprout,

You should try it out.

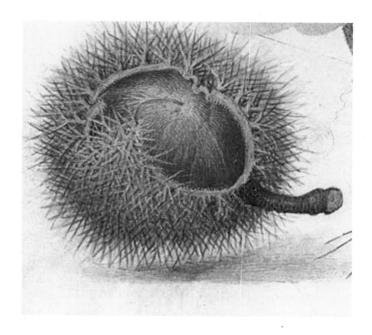

Elder

Where would we be?

Without the Elder tree.

With its white posy,

Such a fragrant beauty.

ELDER.

Sureau. Holunder.

Birch

White like paper, The skin starts to flake,

And if you scrape her, Tinder you can make.

A sugar replacement, and a chewing gum,

Xylitol mixed with mint, can't wait to try some.

If in Spring you carve a tap, with hammer and nail give
a whack,

A refreshing drink is its sap, just make sure to plug the
crack.

Yes the silver birch, has many uses,

Do some research, on all the things it produces.

My Little Olive Sapling

Leaves of silver green,

Make tea with no caffeine,

This one has Gods blessing,

My little olive sapling,

Someday I hope it gives,

Lots of tasty olives,

For Italians I know,

In pizza, pasta, bread,

You often find them spread,

The amazing olive tree,

Making things yummy.

Pine

Why only at Christmas, do you use us?

Don't you know, if you don't throw,

Away your pine trees, it can cure your sneeze?

Full of vitamin C and totally free,

Pine needles of evergreen,

Can always be seen.

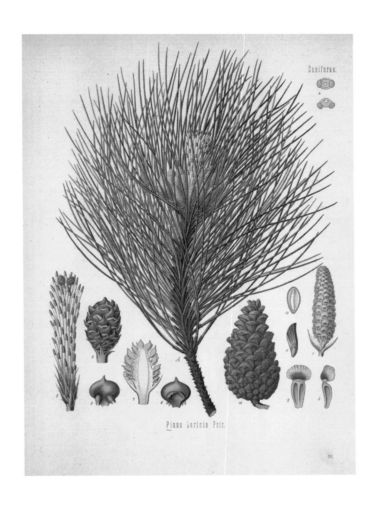

Carbon Dioxide

Each and every tree,

Gives their gifts to me,

What a bargain,

Breathing in my garden,

They take carbon in,

And give out oxygen,

So its life they give,

Without them we can't live.

If you want to breathe,

Plant trees to win,

Don't forget to feed,

Them with carbon.

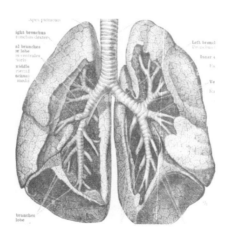

Apple Trees

Keep your eyes up high,

Apples you might spy,

If on them you stumble,

You can make a crumble,

Some might choose,

With sugar to infuse,

For apple cider vinegar,

Pureed for another.

In barrels one brews,

Drinks for adults to amuse.

But always with my supply,

I make an apple pie.

The Circle of Life

If a log falls down,

Let it stay,

Do not frown,

It will decay,

And become a fungus town,

Bugs will dance ballet,

When its wet and brown,

Frogs will come to play,

And as it rots down,

Other tree roots will buffet,

Leave it on the ground,

All will be okay.

Cherry

Here is something,

Something very merry,

It's a sweet thing,

Take all that you can carry,

In the basket that you bring,

To collect this berry,

Towards the end of Spring,

A juicy ruby cherry.

Possibilities

When a child sees,

A bunch of trees,

They see possibilities,

Helicopters instead of keys,

Bullets not berries,

A hotel for honeybees,

A spear for playing Hercules,

A game of hide and freeze,

And even fairy parties,

Up in those wishing trees.

Yew

As I walked one morn,

Through the early dew,

A golden ray of sun,

With a coloured hue,

From the cloud was born,

And landed on a yew,

I watched it through some corn,

A beauty seen by few.

Fig

I got a little twig,

From my neighbours fig,

With my shovel I did dig,

To plant that little twig,

Wow it grew so big.

Figue de Bordeaux violet

Health

One day I met a bee,

Heres what he said to me,

If you want to be,

Happy and healthy,

Heres a tip for free,

Daily take pine needle tea,

And sit beneath a tree.

Printed in Great Britain
by Amazon

46879832R00023